Say NO to BULLYING

written by
Louise Spilsbury

illustrated by
Mike Gordon

BARRON'S

Editor: Victoria Brooker
Design: Basement68

All inquiries should be addressed to:
Barron's Educational Series, Inc.
250 Wireless Boulevard
Hauppauge, NY 11788
www.barronseduc.com

ISBN: 978-1-4380-0401-3

Library of Congress Control No.: 2013946363

Date of Manufacture: November 2013
Manufactured by: WKT Co. Ltd., Shenzhen, Guandong, China

Printed in China
9 8 7 6 5 4 3 2 1

Contents

What is bullying?

Bullying is any kind of behavior that hurts you or makes you feel scared, unhappy, or uncomfortable. Some bullies bully others by pushing them around or by physically hurting and injuring them. Some bullies tease, insult, or threaten their targets. Others spread cruel rumors online. There are many forms of bullying and all of them are unsafe and unacceptable. Bullying is not okay and we should all say NO to it!

▼ Bullying can and does happen to lots of different people.

Bullying basics

There are so many different ways of bullying that sometimes people don't realize they are being bullied; they just know that someone is making them unhappy. If a person or group of people call you names, pinch or hurt you, spread lies about you, scare you, send you mean texts, leave you out of conversations or games, make you feel embarrassed or take your things, then you are being bullied. People can be bullied in many other ways, too. Recognizing the different forms of bullying is one of the first steps in tackling it.

Did You Know?

There are no hard and fast rules, but bullying is usually:
• something someone does to hurt you—it's on purpose
• something that upsets you and makes you feel helpless
• something bad that someone does or says to you more than once

Spot the signs

Bullying affects people in different ways. It can make people feel lonely, unhappy, and frightened. It can make them feel angry and violent. It can make them lose confidence or think there is something wrong with them. It may make them ill. Bullying can even lead to people harming themselves as a way of letting their feelings out or escaping.

If any of the things listed below describes you or things that happen to you, you may be being bullied.

- Lost interest in your favorite activities?
- Had things taken from you at school?
- Lost or changed friends a lot?
- Don't feel like joining in with people or activities?
- Feel nervous and lack confidence?
- Sometimes come home with bruises and scratches?
- Have headaches, stomach aches, or other physical symptoms?
- Have trouble keeping up with schoolwork?
- Have problems eating or sleeping, or even find you're wetting the bed?
- Feel unusually sad, moody, anxious, lonely, or depressed?

YOU CAN DO IT!

Know your feelings and trust them, too. If you feel upset, it is likely that there is a good reason for it. Recognize the warning signs of bullying and do something about it before it does too much damage.

▶ Feelings are like a fire alarm. They go off to tell us when something is wrong! If someone makes you feel unhappy, then your feelings are telling you something's wrong and you need to do something about it.

Saying "No"

One of the things that makes it so hard to say no to bullying is that targets of bullying often feel alone. They might think that they are the only ones being bullied, or that no one else understands how they feel or gets what it is like to be them.

You're not alone

Some people think there's no choice but to accept the things that are happening to them, and that they just have to learn to put up with it. Not so! Bullying is not something we can or should ignore and it's absolutely critical to remember you are not alone if you are being bullied. Nearly everyone is, has been, or will be bullied at some point in their lives by people at school, by brothers or sisters, or by adults. There are many other people like you that face bullying every day.

▼ Bullying can make you feel alone and powerless. It can make you feel trapped in your own world sometimes. You are not alone. There are people who care and people who can help.

Did You Know?

A recent study done in the U.K. found that about one quarter of all students are bullied at some point in their school lives, and another study found that fear of bullying was a serious issue for more than half of them.

Taking the first steps

If you're being bullied it can be hard to believe that you can do something about it. After all, you don't have much of a choice about where you live, go to school, or even go out to play soccer or meet friends. And because bullies push you around, you probably feel utterly powerless, too. But you can do something about bullying—and you're already taking the first steps by reading this book. You can learn and practice things to do in different situations and how to get other people involved when you need to. You can also try to change things and sort out the situation so that the bullying stops.

YOU CAN DO IT!

You can turn things around—just look at all the other people who've been bullied but turned out fine. Famous soccer player David Beckham was bullied: "There was a bullying side to starting sport so young. Because you're not going out, on the Monday at school, people would be like, 'You stayed in, you played football [soccer].' But I bumped into those same people and they were like, 'Can we come and watch you play?'"

◀ Bullying is horrible and very serious, but it can be stopped and there will be brighter, happier times ahead.

Types of bullying

There are different types of bullying. Some are less obvious than others. Sometimes things happen that upset, scare, or embarrass us, but they are not bullying. When you know about the different types of bullying, you can be prepared to say "No" to bullying if and when it starts.

When a friend is a bully

Sadly, some friends can be bullies. If a friend does things like constantly put you down, says mean things, bosses you around, makes you feel bad for seeing other people, or makes you do things you don't want to, they are not a true friend. They are bullying you. Being bullied by a friend is very hurtful and hard to deal with because you feel betrayed and upset. When a so-called friend is being unkind to you deliberately, it is time to make some new friends.

YOU CAN DO IT!

A friend who is a bully is really difficult to spot, but it's important to be able to tell the difference between a real friend and a fake one. A real friend is someone who treats you with the same kindness you show to them.

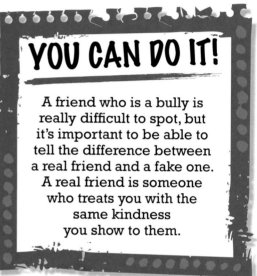

▶ A real friend wouldn't do things to hurt you, like use your secrets (such as a fear of spiders) to upset you.

Dealing with a bully-friend

Here are some things you can try if a friend is bullying you:

- You could give them the chance to change. Tell them clearly and calmly that their behavior is not okay with you.
- Avoid them when they bully. Some people are fun to be with sometimes, like when you are alone with them, but bully at other times, like when you are in a group. You can choose when to hang out with someone and when not to.
- Find friends who are real friends. They may not seem to be as interesting as the bully you know, but once you get to know them they may be fun.
- End the friendship. You could gradually reduce the amount of time you spend with them and make excuses for why you can't see them until you are hardly together. Or, tell them straight out that the friendship is over because of the way they bully you and make you feel.

▶ If a real friend upsets or offends you, they say sorry or at least do something to show you they are sorry—and they mean it. Bullies don't.

Did You Know?

It's not always bullying when a friend makes us feel upset or hurt. For example, friends sometimes say nasty or hurtful things to each other in the heat of an argument. The difference is that real friends usually say sorry and make up pretty quickly afterward.

Teasing and name-calling

Teasing people and calling them names to hurt their feelings is bullying. For example, a bully might taunt someone about the way they look, say rude things about them when they walk past, or make up a nasty nickname to shout out when they see them. Teasing and name-calling can hurt people badly.

▼ Jokes are funny and make us laugh. Teasing and name-calling hurt our feelings. You only need to see someone's reactions to know the difference.

When teasing is bullying

Have you heard phrases like this before?: "Don't be so sensitive—I was only kidding." "What's wrong with you—can't you take a joke?" If someone ridicules you in a way that you don't think is funny, keeps trying to make you look foolish, or generally mocks and taunts you, it can be really hurtful. If you are being teased and you don't like it, then teasing has crossed the line and become bullying. It doesn't make any difference if the bully claims they were only joking. If you feel their comments were hurtful and not funny, it was not a joke and it is not a laughing matter.

Did You Know?

Some people tease others because they think they are being funny. They may not be trying to bully you. It is time to tell them that they need to learn a new way to make people laugh that doesn't involve hurting your or other people's feelings.

▼ Almost half of all the bullying that happens in schools involves teasing, taunting, name-calling, and insults. Some people try to imagine that they have an invisible force field around them that the words bounce off of so they barely hear them.

Saying no to name-calling

Name-calling is a type of verbal bullying that is easier to spot than teasing, but it is no easier to deal with. Insults don't physically hurt you, but being bullied like this can make people feel really unhappy, sometimes for years after it has happened. When someone calls you bad names it can even start to make you feel that there is something wrong with you when there isn't. It can be very difficult to ignore nasty comments, but it's important that you don't let them get to you or make you believe that they are right. You should never put yourself down, no matter what others say.

YOU CAN DO IT!

If a bully makes nasty comments about the way you look, think what advice you'd give to a friend in that situation. If a bully told your friend she was too tall or too thin, you would probably tell her that the bully was wrong and was exaggerating about her appearance just to be mean. Well, try saying that to yourself, too.

Relationship bullying

Relationship bullying is when a bully tries to harm your relationships with other people, for example by leaving you out of games or groups. It's very hurtful because although one person usually leads this type of bullying, other people either join in or let it happen, so it can feel like everyone is ganging up on you.

How it happens

Relationship bullying can happen in different ways. For example, a bully might invite everyone else to come to a party except you, or they might persuade other people to stop talking to you, or they pretend they don't hear you talking when you speak. Another type of relationship bullying is when a group of people roll their eyes, make faces, or make rude noises every time a person walks past. This makes the target feel like everyone else is talking about them or laughing at them.

▲ Relationship bullying can be silent and secretive and hard for other people, such as teachers, to see, but it is a very serious and harmful form of bullying.

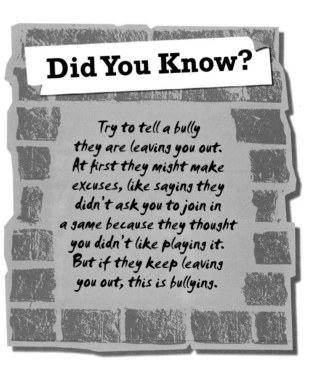

Did You Know?

Try to tell a bully they are leaving you out. At first they might make excuses, like saying they didn't ask you to join in a game because they thought you didn't like playing it. But if they keep leaving you out, this is bullying.

Feeling left out

When a bully excludes you and persuades or bullies other people into doing the same, it can make you feel very alone. It can even make you think that no one likes you. We're all different and it's perfectly understandable that some people won't have much in common with you or won't want to be great friends with you, but that's no excuse for a bully or anyone else to exclude you on purpose. Although it might feel like everybody is against you, they aren't. Nice people often go along with a bully because they are scared of being shunned too, or because they are afraid to stand up to the bully. It doesn't mean they don't like you. In fact, they probably feel bad or ashamed of what's happening and would be friendly toward you if it weren't for the bully.

YOU CAN DO IT!

Don't be a bystander to bullying. If you stand by and keep quiet when someone is being left out, then you are supporting the bully. Maybe you don't like the person who is the victim or maybe the bully is a friend. That's no excuse. People need to stand up and try to stop bullying from happening, for example by saying something to the bully or to an adult and getting others to say something, too.

▼ It would be great if people would speak up to stop someone from being left out. Would you speak up and say something like: "Give him a chance?"

Physical bullying

Physical bullying is any physical contact that can hurt or injure a person, like hitting, kicking, punching, scratching, or shoving. It also includes damaging someone's things and threatening to hurt them.

Getting hurt

There's a difference between getting hurt by accident and getting physically bullied. If you're in a playground or on a playing field and someone accidentally slams into you, that's an accident. The person should say sorry and you continue to play. It's a completely different situation if someone does something deliberately like punching you, shoving you into a wall as you walk down a hallway, or keeps pinching you. These things are forms of physical bullying.

▶ If someone repeatedly pulls your hair, pokes, or pinches you, that is physical bullying. It doesn't matter that it's not bruising or injuring you, it is still a serious matter and should be stopped.

Top Tip!

If someone hurts you, don't fight back if you can help it. Most bullies are more used to confrontation than you. If you fight back you could make the situation worse, get badly hurt or be blamed for starting the trouble. Just get out of there and then talk to an adult about it.

Your safety comes first and if you ever get hurt on purpose by someone at school, tell a teacher immediately, and make sure you tell your parents when you get home, too.

Threats of violence

Physical bullying also includes things like clothes-pulling, snatching lunch or books, throwing belongings around, and breaking someone else's things. It's also when someone threatens to hurt you if you don't do what they want, or give them something they want, like your lunch money. Threats of violence may not actually physically hurt you, but it can make you feel just as scared and under attack.

Don't get hurt

Some people fight to keep hold of a phone or lunch money because they think a parent will be angry with them if they don't have it, but it's not worth

Did You Know?

If you take photos of any bruises or other injuries a bully gives you, you can use these as evidence to show that physical bullying is taking place.

risking getting hurt to stop a bully from taking your things. It's best to give into the bully's demands, then tell an adult what happened. Remember—keeping yourself safe is the most important thing to do.

▲ Bullying hurts. It hurts and frightens the targets of bullying and it can make everyone else feel scared, too.

Bullying and prejudice

Bullies pick on people for a variety of reasons, and often for no real reason at all, but when they repeatedly attack someone because of their race, sexuality, religion, or culture, we call it prejudice.

Racist bullying

Bullies often pick on people because of something they perceive as different. So, people who have an aspect of themselves that is more obviously different, such as skin color, or a particular style of clothing because of their religion, can be easy targets for some bullies. Bullies use the same tactics as when they are bullying other people—mocking, name-calling, excluding them, or even attacking them physically.

Bullying outsiders

Bullies also attack those they think of as outsiders, for example Gypsy, Roma or Traveller children or refugees who come to their school. This kind of bullying is also based on prejudice and ignorance and on superficial differences, like the fact a person lives in a mobile home or speaks a different first language. It is difficult enough settling in to a strange new place or school for most children in this situation, and a bully's cruel and hostile behavior makes it even harder.

▲ Racist bullying is taken very seriously. If it happens to you, keep a record of all incidents (with dates, times, witnesses, feelings experienced), even if it seems to be only a minor incident at the time. You can use this as evidence when you take a complaint to a teacher or to a person in authority.

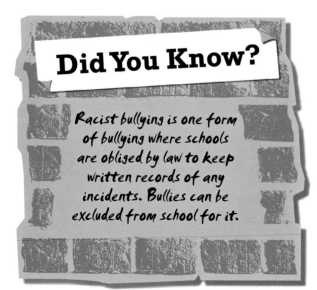

Did You Know?

Racist bullying is one form of bullying where schools are obliged by law to keep written records of any incidents. Bullies can be excluded from school for it.

Homophobic bullying

Homophobic bullying is when someone is bullied because they are accused of being of a different sexual orientation. It often involves using a word like "gay" as an insult, for example if a boy isn't good at football or girls hold hands with each other. There is nothing wrong with being homosexual, and there is nothing wrong with being a boy who doesn't like some of the usual things boys are expected to like. This kind of stereotyping and bullying is wrong and hurtful.

▼ Some boy bullies pick on a boy who doesn't like the same things as them, like football. The bullies may just be jealous because the other boy gets along better with girls than they do.

Top Tip!

Don't use the word "gay" to mean things that are foolish, or to insult someone when they upset you. Even if you don't mean to be unkind or homophobic, using the word "gay" like this isn't allowed in schools because it can make people who are gay feel bad about who they are. Try to challenge stereotypes and stand up to bullying.

Cyberbullying

Cyberbullying is when someone uses the Internet, cell phones, or other interactive and digital technologies to insult, to threaten, spread rumors about, or to upset someone. Most of us use these types of technology every day, but when bullies misuse them, they can be very harmful.

▼ Instead of looking forward to turning on their computer or cell phone, cyberbullying can make people terrified of opening up their messages or hearing the phone ring.

What's different about cyberbullying?

Just like other forms of bullying, cyberbullying can be a one-time thing, like someone distributing a photo to humiliate a target, or it can happen over weeks or months. But, in the past, targets of bullying at school could at least feel safe when they got home. With cyberbullying, bullies can reach their targets 24 hours a day and seven days a week—as soon as victims switch on their cell phone, computer, or game console. Cyberbullying follows victims wherever they go.

Did You Know?

Information circulates at high speed in the digital world. This means that bullies can spread their lies, embarrassing photos, or mean rumors very quickly if they want to. With the click of a button, they can also make sure it reaches a very wide audience immediately, too. The number of bystanders in the cyber world can reach into the millions.

Anonymous attacks

The other difference between cyberbullying and most other forms of bullying is that the bullies are not face to face with their targets. A bully can use false screen names and fake identities, or hide their number so they can send offensive messages or upload upsetting material anonymously.

There are three problems with this. One is that this makes it difficult, though not impossible, to trace the bully. The second problem is that when a bully feels confident they won't get caught, they often get even nastier. They may do or say things that they would not normally do in public.

There have been examples of bullies who call someone names in a playground, then extend this to sending death threats when contacting their victim online or by cell phone. The third problem is that the victim is left wondering who the cyberbully is. This can cause a great deal of stress, for example if they have to go to school wondering each time they see someone, that it could be the person who threatened them anonymously the night before.

YOU CAN DO IT!

Cyberbullies think they can be anonymous, but each time someone sends an e-mail, it leaves an electronic trail that can often be traced back to the sender. Also, all activity that takes place in cyberspace is printable, so victims can save and print offensive messages as proof of what is taking place.

▲ Some people who would never bully other people in real life, turn into cyberbullies online. Perhaps it's because they can't see the impact they are having on people, or because they think they can hide behind a cloak of anonymity.

Cell phone abuse

Cell phone bullying involves sending someone nasty or threatening instant messages, text messages, or calls. All forms of cell phone bullying are upsetting, and some forms, such as "happy slapping," are actually a criminal offense.

Bullying by cell phones

Bullies use cell phones in different ways. Sometimes bullies call someone up and say nasty things to them, or even threaten to hurt or attack them in order to frighten them. Some bullies dial a number and then stay silent on the other end of the phone, to irritate, scare, or confuse the target of their bullying. Bullies also send text messages to scare, upset, or hurt someone on purpose, often anonymously. Bullies may also send embarrassing or private pictures of someone to other people via cell phones.

And even worse, bullies sometimes use cell phones to record vicious acts of bullying. They may hit or attack someone, create a video of the act on their cell phone, and then share the video with their friends. If you are a victim of this type of bullying, get away as quickly as you can to a safe place. Then, tell a parent or another adult who you trust and contact the police. This is a serious crime and it should be dealt with by proper authorities.

▼ You can report cell phone bullying to the police. Police can trace the sender of abusive cell phone texts even if they've hidden their number. Making offensive calls is a crime and if found guilty people may have to pay a large fine or even go to jail.

What to do

There are several things you can do to avoid or stop cell phone bullying:

- Only give your cell phone number out to people you already know and trust.
- Don't answer calls from a private number, or a number you don't know.
- Never reply to text messages from people you don't know, or to any text or video messages that are nasty or rude. By not replying, the bully may think that you didn't receive the message, or that you saw it but that it didn't bother you.
- Report any incidents of bullying to your cell phone company. Check the company's website for information on how to report bullying.

- Protect your friends too—don't give out their numbers without their permission.
- Don't take or send pictures of friends without their permission. You can't control where they end up, who sees them, or what other people might do with them.

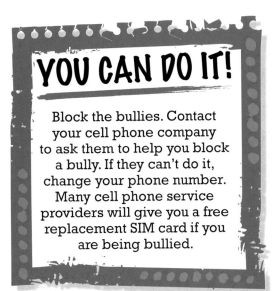

YOU CAN DO IT!

Block the bullies. Contact your cell phone company to ask them to help you block a bully. If they can't do it, change your phone number. Many cell phone service providers will give you a free replacement SIM card if you are being bullied.

▼ Don't leave your cell phone lying around, in case someone picks it up and opens it to steal your number, or send messages to other people that they pretend are from you.

Internet abuse

Bullies attack people via the Internet, too. Some cyberbullies send abusive e-mails and instant messages, or they set up websites that ridicule someone. Some bullies send nasty comments and abuse others via chat rooms. Some even deliberately send viruses or hacking programs that can destroy another person's computer, or delete personal information from their hard drive.

Bullying by websites

One example of Internet bullying is when bullies set up websites to bully others. These often contain pictures and words, and can be very nasty and upsetting for the victims. Bullies might also set up polling sites, where bullies get others to vote, for example, for the ugliest, fattest, or stupidest person at school. In these cases, you could ask the website administrator to remove or disable the sites.

▲ You can get some really good anti-virus programs to make sure you don't get any viruses on your computer that a bully might send through.

Chat room bullying

In Internet chat rooms, a bully might work alone, or several people might gang up on one or more of the members. The fastest way to end the bullying in a chat room is to leave the room. Try to learn how to save a copy of the conversation, as this may be useful if you want to report a bully. Consider setting up private, invitation-only chat rooms for you and your friends. That way if a bully gets in you should find it easier to identify and block them.

Did You Know?

Don't reply to nasty e-mails or abusive postings on chat rooms. Responding when you're upset can make things worse, and some bullies will give up after a few tries if they don't get a reaction.

How to stop cyberbullies

If someone bullies you online, log out immediately or change your screen name. If you've used a nickname in chat rooms, bullies can't track you down via e-mail. Save or print copies of chats, screenshots, e-mails, or blogs that involve bullies. This may be useful if you want to report the bully. For example, if you're being bullied by someone sending you mean e-mails, you can complain to your e-mail service provider. You can also use blocking software to keep bullies out.

It's really important to tell your parents about online bullying, but some people don't because they fear that their parents will simply stop them from using the computer in order to protect them.

YOU CAN DO IT!

Keep your personal information secret.
• Avoid using your real name as a username in a chat room, on instant messenger accounts or as part of your e-mail address.
• Don't mention your address, telephone number, cell phone number, private e-mail address, or upload pictures, even if people ask you to.

Explain your fears to your parents and how important it is to stay connected to your friends in this way. If you can talk about this with them, you should be able to get the bullying stopped and continue to use the Internet, too.

▼ You can set up private chat rooms to keep the bully out.

Social networking sites

Social networking sites, like Facebook, MySpace, and Bebo, are places where you can create a profile about yourself. You can include likes and dislikes, music, videos, and photos that other people can comment on. You can send messages and comments to other people, too. Some people use social networks to bully others.

Did You Know?

If a bully hacks into your Facebook or other accounts and posts offensive images to your profiles, you should tell an adult who you trust and report it to the service provider immediately.

Posting on profiles

People bully others on social networking sites in different ways. They might post insulting messages on your profile wall, add nasty comments to a picture you've uploaded, or put a bad or embarrassing photo of you on their own profile that makes you look silly, and then get their friends to send it to others.

Some bullies steal personal information and photos of people from social networking sites so they can set up fake profiles and pretend to be that person. Then they can send nasty messages to others who may believe that the messages are really from you.

▼ Be smart and keep your passwords to social network and all other sites top secret. And I mean TOP secret!

24

Social networking safety

Here are some tips on how to be safe when using social networking sites:

• Set up privacy settings to control who can see different parts of your profile, like your photos.

• Only add friends who you really trust and who you know in the real world.

• Trust your instincts. If someone you don't quite trust sends you a friend request, ignore it.

• Never join in with posting comments or making fun of someone on a social networking site. If you do, you are taking part in the cyberbullying.

• If you ever see a fake profile that has been made to humiliate or taunt someone, you should report it.

YOU CAN DO IT!

Think carefully about what you put on social networking sites. Don't reveal too much or say things that you wouldn't want everyone to know. Once information is online, it's easy for other people to read it. More and more bullies are using information they find on Facebook and other sites against their targets.

▼ Some people choose to post a picture they like or a photo of their favorite animal or band instead of a photo of themselves on their profile page, so bullies cannot steal their photo or make rude comments about it.

When adults are bullies

Most of the bullying that happens to young people is done by other young people, but sometimes adults can be bullies. For example, while the vast majority of teachers and coaches who work with young people in schools and sports clubs are caring and kind, a few are bullies.

▶ When teachers bully, it can suggest to other young people that this is an acceptable way to behave. It isn't.

Teacher troubles

When a teacher is a bully, they use their position of power to criticize, punish, or embarrass a student in unreasonable ways. For example, they may insult a student or hurt their feelings by making nasty comments about them, their appearance, background, personality, or schoolwork. They might try to embarrass or humiliate them in front of classmates, give them low marks unfairly, or even threaten to hit them. If you feel that a teacher is bullying you, it's a very serious issue and one you need to resolve.

Top Tip!

It's not bullying if a teacher criticizes you or your work fairly or gives you extra homework or a detention after you have done something wrong. These things might upset or anger you, but discipline and constructive criticism are important parts of school life and you just have to accept them.

Tackling teachers

Bullying is wrong no matter how old the person is who is bullying you. If you're feeling threatened or intimidated by a teacher, you need to talk to your parents or another teacher you trust. Many students are worried about reporting a teacher, or any other adult who is in a position of authority, because they fear it could lead to more bullying by that teacher, or another punishment like low grades or missing out on special activities.

▶ It's your teacher's job to look after you. You have a right not to be made to feel stupid, be called names, or be punished unfairly. Talk to your parents or an adult you trust so you can resolve the situation.

Asking for help

If you're worried, ask your parents to introduce the topic to your teacher in an indirect way. For example, they could meet him or her and say: "I'm worried. My son seems afraid of coming to class. Do you know what's going on? Is someone in class bullying him?" Hopefully the teacher will realize what they have been doing is wrong and stop. If the situation doesn't improve, you and your parents have to take it further, to the principal, or even to local authorities (police) if necessary.

Did You Know?

Adults can bully other adults, too. Bullying happens in the places where adults work, such as offices.

Parents who bully

It may seem strange to think that parents can be bullies, but they can be. Some parents enforce rules with too heavy a hand, and others constantly belittle their children. Parents are only human and make mistakes, but some behave in ways that are inappropriate.

Hurting at home

Some parent bullies regularly insult or hurt their children, or use threats of violence like: "Sit down before I slap you" to make them do as they are told. No form of discipline should be nasty or violent, and treating people like this can make them feel scared and lonely.

Other parents don't mean to bully. They think they are motivating you when they say things that upset you, like teasing you for being chubby to get you to exercise more or comparing you unfavorably to a sibling by saying things like: "why don't you work harder, then you could be more like your sister?" These parents may not mean to be unkind, but when you hear comments like this a lot, it can make you feel miserable and worthless.

◀ If a parent constantly puts you down, it can make you feel unloved and shrink your self-confidence.

Talking to parents

Dealing with a parent bully is very difficult, but it's important that the parent bullying be stopped. The first thing you should try is to talk to the parent. This often works right away if a parent hasn't meant to be unkind. If you calmly and clearly explain how their behavior makes you feel, without insulting them or getting angry, they should listen and understand what you say.

If that doesn't work, or if you are too scared to talk directly to your parents, or you're convinced it won't help, then it's a good idea to talk to another adult you trust. This could be someone else in your family, like a grandparent, or aunt or uncle, or you could ask a teacher at school for help.

▶ Sometimes parents ask or tell you to do things that you don't want to, like clean your room. This is not bullying! Sometimes it's best to do as parents suggest, or they'll be justifiably annoyed.

When bullying becomes abuse

When an adult bullies a child or young person by hitting or hurting them, this is physical abuse. When an adult bullies a young person into taking part in any kind of sexual activity this is sexual abuse. Both kinds of abuse are a criminal offense.

Keeping safe

Your body belongs to you, and only you have the right to decide what happens to it and who touches it. If someone hits or harms you in a way that hurts or frightens you, or if someone older than you tries to touch you, or makes you watch or do something that feels wrong or that you don't like, tell them to stop. Try to say this loudly and clearly and then go and tell an adult who you trust about it.

▶ Nobody has the right to hurt or abuse you.

Did You Know?

If you are too frightened of an abuser to say no, you may feel forced to do what the abuser says, in order to keep safe. You must tell someone about what happened later. This is never something to feel bad about. It's not your fault. The most important thing is to keep safe.

Taking action

Some people are reluctant to take action and speak out when the abuser is someone they care about. They worry about what will happen to that person. But if people we care about hurt us, it doesn't necessarily mean that the person is all bad. It just means that they have a problem, for example an alcohol or drug addiction, and that they need help.

The best way to get the help you both need, is to tell an adult you trust and keep telling different adults until someone does something to make the problem stop. In the long run, this will help you and help the adult who is doing the abusing.

▼ Some things are really tough to tell, but it's vital that you do. If the first adult you tell about the abuse doesn't believe you or help you, then you need to keep finding other adults to tell until someone does.

Why do people bully?

Many different types of people can be bullies and there are many reasons why they do it. Some bullies don't know how hurtful their actions can be. Others don't care about other people's feelings and do it to feel powerful. Some do it because they have been treated badly themselves.

Bullying to boost yourself

Many bullies look for attention and try to make themselves feel more important. When they taunt and mock someone, other people may laugh, and that makes them feel more popular. When they push and hit and make someone feel afraid of them, they feel tougher, cooler, or more powerful.

Some bullies are spoiled at home and expect everyone to do what they say or want. Other bullies are jealous of the person they are bullying and put them down to feel better about themselves. Some people join in or go along with the bullying of others to save themselves from being bullied.

▼ Bullies come in all shapes and sizes, but one thing they often have in common is that something or someone is making them feel bad about themselves, so they bully others to make themselves feel better.

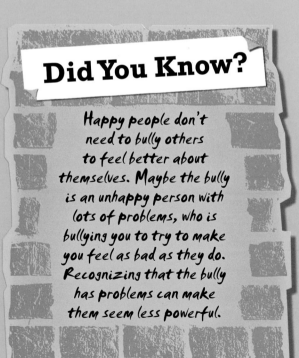

Bullies with big problems

Bullying is bad, bad, bad and there is never any excuse for people to do it, but the fact is that some young people become bullies because they have serious problems of their own. Some people become bullies because they are upset by something, like the death of a loved one or their parents' divorce. They use bullying as a way of taking out their anger or unhappiness on someone else. Some bullies come from families that shout, insult, and push each other around all the time, so the bully thinks that this is a normal way to behave. Some bullies have been badly bullied themselves by someone in the past and are making up for it by copying that behavior and doing the same thing to others.

▲ Bullies have often been, or are being, bullied themselves, but even if you are bullied, you have a choice—you don't have to turn into a bully, too.

Did You Know?

Happy people don't need to bully others to feel better about themselves. Maybe the bully is an unhappy person with lots of problems, who is bullying you to try to make you feel as bad as they do. Recognizing that the bully has problems can make them seem less powerful.

Say no to being a bully

In the end, bullying makes everyone miserable—including the bully. Bullies are often feared rather than liked by other people, and they end up losing friends as they get older. They can be suspended or expelled from school if they are reported to a teacher, or punished by the police if they physically hurt someone.

You can change

The good news is that you can change. You don't have to continue being a bully. Some people just decide to stop and don't do it anymore. They may even say sorry to the person they've been bullying and try to be friendlier toward them. It may take a while for people to trust you again, but you can help this by trying to cooperate more with other people, for example, by sometimes doing what they want, not just what you want. You could also watch people who get along with others without bullying and learn from the way they behave.

Did You Know?

People who bully others are more likely to:
- get into fights and drop out of school
- have problems with alcohol and other drugs
- grow into adults who bully
- be convicted of crimes.

▼ If you've been a bully, think about how you would feel if someone was doing the same to you or to someone you like. Is that really the person you want to be?

34

Figure out why you bully

If you find it hard to stop being a bully, think about what's going on in your life to make you so unhappy that you take it out on others. Do you bully because you are being bullied yourself? If so, you need to deal with that situation instead of being a bully. If you bully because it makes you feel more confident and powerful, think of other activities to make yourself feel good. Learning and being good at a new skill or sport will give you a better buzz than pushing other people around.

Ask for help

Some people worry they'll be punished if they admit they have been bullying someone, but this isn't so. If you're asking for help, you will get it. Try talking to a parent or teacher, or call a bullying helpline.

Top Tip!

Practice being nicer to and more positive about other people. Set yourself the goal of complimenting three people every day. You could find something good to say about their sporting skills, shoes, or test scores. You should find you get a much friendlier response in return.

▼ No one's expecting bullies to turn into angels overnight, but they can change their ways.

Learn to be more bully-proof

Even if some bullies eventually change their ways, there will always be new bullies. While targets of bullying are absolutely, 100 percent NOT responsible for being bullied, there are a few things they can do to appear, and become, more confident so a bully might think twice before picking on them. If you can learn to be more bully-proof, you might be able to stop bullies before they even get started.

◄ Fake it till you make it! Faking confidence won't stop every bully, but it should prevent some from bullying you.

Fake confidence

Bullies sometimes pick on people who seem vulnerable, who look like they could be easily hurt by a mean comment. People will bother you less if you walk, sit, and act confident. Some people just seem to be born confident. Others have to learn it like any other skill.

Top Tip!

Many people believe that if you do something for six weeks it becomes a habit, and after that you'll do it without thinking. If you keep practicing how to fake confidence, one day you should just look and feel more confident without having to force it.

How it's done

The way we hold our bodies when we sit, stand, and walk gives signals to other people. Someone who slouches and hunches looks smaller and more vulnerable than someone who walks tall. Someone who hugs their arms over their body, as if to protect themselves, looks nervous or shy. To look more confident (even if you don't feel it!) try to hold your body straight (as if you are one straight line from head to feet). Walk with a purpose, as if you know where you are going and what you are doing next, even if you don't. It also helps to keep your hands away from your face and avoid fidgeting when you're sitting down.

▼ Faking confidence takes a lot of practice—try it in front of the mirror and in situations where you feel at ease.

You could put your hands in your pockets so you don't start clenching them nervously. Try to keep your head up and look around calmly rather than looking down at the ground.

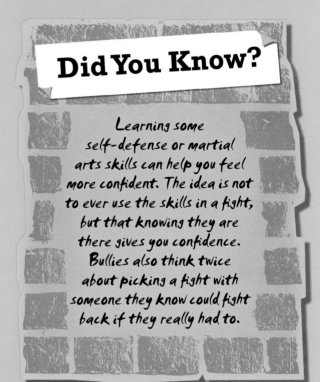

Did You Know?

Learning some self-defense or martial arts skills can help you feel more confident. The idea is not to ever use the skills in a fight, but that knowing they are there gives you confidence. Bullies also think twice about picking a fight with someone they know could fight back if they really had to.

Feel good about yourself

Faking confidence isn't easy. It's much easier to look confident on the outside when you feel good about yourself on the inside. Feeling good about yourself is important for everyone, but it's also a useful shield against potential bullies.

▶ Feeling good about yourself can be like wearing a bully-proof vest—it won't stop people from making mean comments, but it will help you feel like you have a protective shield.

Believe in yourself!

The first step on the road to self-confidence is focusing on what's good about you. Instead of thinking about the things you're not good at or the things you don't like about yourself, focus on the good things. What are you good at? What are your good points? Write them down and read them every day! Learn to accept the things you cannot change, like your height or shoe size. After all, no one's perfect. Learn to be proud of your differences. When you believe in yourself, bullies won't be able to make you think that there is something wrong with you when there isn't. And if you know and accept your shortcomings, it isn't going to hurt your feelings when someone else rudely points them out.

YOU CAN DO IT!

A good tactic is to turn the unkind things people say into positives. For example, "Yes, I know I'm not good at basketball, but you should see me swim!" Or try "Oh, I really like them" if someone criticizes your shoes.

Give it a try

You can talk yourself into being more self-confident, but what makes a real difference is getting out there and trying new things or doing the things you like more often. Why not join a club, take up a new hobby, or practice a game or skill until you're really good at it?

Some things might be scary or challenging at first, like joining a drama group to put on a show, but when you do things like this you feel good about yourself. Do the things you enjoy more, too. Get on your bike, go out to the movies or visit your friend's house. When you're busy and getting a real sense of achievement from your day, you're less likely to let one stupid comment from a bully spoil it for you.

▲ What sport do you play? We all need to factor some fun, physical time into our day. It makes us feel healthier and better about ourselves.

Did You Know?

Did you know that doing exercise boosts serotonin and endorphins? These are chemicals in the body that make you feel good about yourself. Exercising also makes you healthier and helps your circulation, (blood flow around your body) making you look brighter and better, too.

Learn some responses

Another way to be more bully-proof is to brainstorm some responses for those times when people say something hurtful. Maybe the person didn't mean to be hurtful, but it's a good idea to get used to saying when you don't like something. It shows people that you know you deserve to be treated properly, and that you're not someone who is going to put up with being treated badly.

▼ Work on your responses with someone in your family. You could ask them to say things you've practiced answers for already. Or get them to make up new put downs so you can practice using some of your stock responses.

Comeback clues

Use a comeback to say something firmly and clearly, not to say something nasty in return. That makes things worse, not better. State facts such as: "That's not funny. Please don't say that again" or "I don't like it when you say mean things like that." You might need to practice responses to their responses, too. If the person replies: "Can't you take a joke?" you could say: "I can take a joke, but being hurtful to people isn't funny."

Top Tip!

If you find that you get really angry if people make a mean remark, find better ways to vent your anger than insulting them back. You could write them a really angry letter about how you feel, and then throw it away!

Be included

You could also practice some responses for when someone tries to leave you out of a game or event. Ask why they do it and be ready with some answers. If they say: "You're not good enough!" say: "I'll get better when I practice!" If they say: "There are too many people playing already" say: "There's always room for one more." Try to stay cheerful rather than sounding hurt or irritated, but be persistent. Don't give up!

Be safe

Using responses that you've practiced can work with many people, but it might make some people angry. If someone who seems threatening says something to you, especially if there is no adult around who can help you to stay safe, the best thing to do is to say nothing and if possible, leave.

▶ Listen to your body. Avoid using clever comebacks if your body is warning you that someone could turn nasty. Put your personal safety first.

Did You Know?

Your body sends you signals when you feel anxious or unsafe. If you feel butterflies in your stomach, get sweaty palms, or your heart starts beating faster, take notice. If you're feeling unsafe it is time to leave, not to use a clever comeback.

41

The power of friends

Friends help make you more bully-proof. When you have friends that believe in you, it helps you to feel good about yourself, too. There's safety in numbers, as well. Bullies tend to pick on people who are alone, so having a few good friends with you most of the time is another good way of keeping them away.

Friendly bully beaters

Never underestimate the power of friends. Good friends are there to share fun times, but they also help us when something goes wrong. When you have real friends, you have someone to talk to if a bully says or does something mean. This can stop you from feeling alone. Friends can remind you that what the bully says isn't true or doesn't matter. When you have good friends, you know you're not the failure that a bully might be trying to make you out to be.

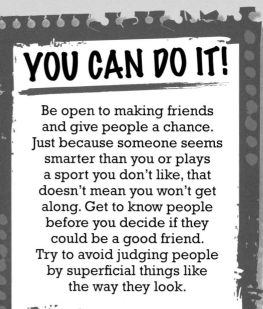

YOU CAN DO IT!

Be open to making friends and give people a chance. Just because someone seems smarter than you or plays a sport you don't like, that doesn't mean you won't get along. Get to know people before you decide if they could be a good friend. Try to avoid judging people by superficial things like the way they look.

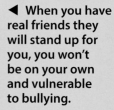

◄ When you have real friends they will stand up for you, you won't be on your own and vulnerable to bullying.

Making and keeping friends

There's no magic formula for making friends. Try to join clubs and after-school activities to meet people. Ask new people about themselves and listen to the answers so they know you're genuinely interested in what they're saying. Chat about things like music, TV shows, movies, or sports. When you make a good friend, work at keeping them. Spend time with them and notice when they are down. Help them if they need it. Be someone they can trust. Don't tell secrets they share with you to anyone else or talk about them behind their back. If you are a good friend, people are more likely to be good friends to you.

Top Tip!

If things don't work out with a potential friend, stay friendly toward that person anyway. Don't bad-mouth them or tell secrets they told you, or you will become someone that no one wants to know.

▶ Try to be a good friend to others, including those who don't seem to have many friends. If you see someone sitting alone, try to start a conversation with them. Friendly people make more friends.

Dealing with bullies

When you are being bullied, you might feel helpless and think there's nothing you can do about it. That's not so. There are things you can do to deal with bullies. You can learn strategies to help you cope in certain situations, and you can take action to stop the bully from hurting you.

Avoid the bully

One way to deal with a bully is to avoid him or her. Reduce their chances of bullying you again by keeping out of their way and out of their reach. Change seats to be farther away from them in class and leave the room—if you can—when they come in.

Avoid places where bullying happens, like quiet bathrooms or dark corners of a playground where teachers cannot see. Try to stay with friends or people you trust—bullies are less likely to approach you if you're in a group of people who'll back you up.

▲ It makes sense to stay out of a bully's way or to stay in sight of people who can stop the bullying if it starts.

YOU CAN DO IT!

Be aware of what's going on around you to avoid being found alone by a bully.
• Speed up so you aren't the last one in the locker room.
• Don't hang out at school after everyone else has left.
• Go to the bathroom with a friend or when it's busy there.

Ignore the bully

No one should ignore bullying, but it is worth trying to ignore the bully. There's an important difference. The idea is to ignore the bully at the moment when they insult, makes faces, or shove you, in order to get yourself away from a sticky situation. Try to turn and walk away, remembering to hold your head up high and look confident as you do so. Don't worry if the bully tries to tease you for "running away." Bullies don't deserve a response or the courtesy of staying around to hear them, and they can't continue to bully you if you're not there.

Top Tip!

Ignore the bully, but don't ignore the bullying. Write down every incident that happens, even if it only seems minor. Keep a diary of when and where it happens, what is said, and how it makes you feel. You can use this as evidence when you report the bullying to an adult.

▶ Ignoring a bully is very hard to do, but try to keep it up. It can work if the bully gets tired or bored of trying to get a reaction from you, such as making you angry or tearful.

Take control

You can't control what a bully says to you, but you can practice controlling how you react to it at that moment. Bullies want to get a reaction from you. Getting a reaction from someone can make bullies feel like they have the power they want.

▶ Focusing on breathing deeply and slowly keeps you calm and stops you from thinking about what the bully is saying, too!

Hide your reactions

When a bully insults or taunts you they are trying to upset, embarrass, or scare you. If you can keep calm and hide your feelings, you are not giving them the reaction they want. You could simply say: "Yeah, whatever..." in a calm, normal tone of voice, while calmly and confidently moving away from them. Try to look at them as if they are not frightening you or upsetting you, even if you don't feel that way inside. This is really hard to do, but if you can practice and pull this off, it really can help. Again, this doesn't mean you are ignoring the bullying. You can and should let out your true feelings when you're at home or somewhere you feel safe later.

YOU CAN DO IT!

Getting oxygen to the brain helps make you feel calm. When you're away from the bully, breathe in slowly and deeply, while counting to five. Then hold your breath for two seconds before breathing out for another five seconds.

Let it go

A bully's cruel words often hurt us long after they have said them. One minute you're walking along, minding your own business and feeling good. Then the bully says something nasty and it brings you crashing down. You don't deserve this. Try reliving incidents in your head, like scenes from a movie, but change the endings. For example, if someone said: "You lost us the game because you're a useless goalie." Imagine that instead of being silent, you replied: "Well, at least I tried" or "We would have won if you scored more goals." Don't let the bully's nasty words bring you down. Change them and make them positive.

Top Tip!

Bullies are good at making people think they deserve to be treated badly. Don't give a bully the satisfaction of getting to you like that. Keep reminding yourself that you're a great person and that we all deserve respect and kindness from others. The bully is the problem, not you.

▼ Take control! If a bully says something rude like: "Those shoes belong in a circus!" say simply, "Well, I like them."

Saying "No"

If ignoring a bully isn't enough to make them stop, telling them to stop may show them that you're not going to put up with their bullying. It might even make them stop. But like all the techniques for dealing with a bully, these need practice until you're confident enough to try them out for real.

Ways with words

When someone keeps on bullying you using words, don't get caught up in arguments about what they said. Their actual words don't deserve a response. Try to look them in the eye and say something you can practice at home like: "That's a mean thing to say. I don't like it" or "Stop making fun of me." Be polite but keep it short and simple. You don't have to say why you want them to stop. Just tell them to stop. Try to say the words you choose in a calm, firm voice, even if you're feeling shaky inside.

Did You Know?

The tone of voice you use when saying "no" is vital. Try to make your voice loud enough to be easily heard, so it doesn't sound too soft and unsure, or too loud and angry. Try to speak clearly and calmly so you don't sound hesitant.

◄ When you want to practice speaking firmly and clearly you could copy the voice that a good teacher uses when they tell someone to stop doing something.

Getting louder

What if someone is bullying you by pushing, tripping, or hitting you? In front of a mirror, practice standing up tall and straight and putting your hands (palms facing outward) up in front of you to make a sort of wall between you and the bully, and say: "No, Stop it!" Practice making this gesture and saying these words clearly and forcefully. Make sure you speak loudly enough to be heard by other people. Then walk or run away immediately.

When you do this for real, the bully may not stop. If when you say "No!" and try to move away they try to stop you from leaving, yell louder. Try to pull away and as you do so, shout: "STOP IT!," "LEAVE ME ALONE!" or "HELP!" Make your yells short, strong, and very loud. Then leave and go straight to an adult for help.

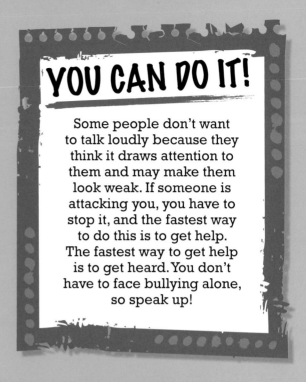

YOU CAN DO IT!

Some people don't want to talk loudly because they think it draws attention to them and may make them look weak. If someone is attacking you, you have to stop it, and the fastest way to do this is to get help. The fastest way to get help is to get heard. You don't have to face bullying alone, so speak up!

▼ If you shout loudly enough, someone should come to help you. Even if this doesn't happen, shouting in the bully's ear should make them drop their guard long enough for you to get away.

Out and about

What about when bullying happens when you're on your way to and from school, or on your way to a friend's house? Bullies can make you feel scared to go out and do things, but it's important to find a way to get to do the things you enjoy and keep in touch with friends.

On the way to school

If you're being bullied on the school bus, try to sit near the front by the bus driver, ideally with friends. Tell your parents what's happening so they can call or write to the school to ask them to take action. You could also ask parents or friends for a ride to and from school until the problem is dealt with.

Did You Know?

If you feel very unsafe while walking to school you could get a personal safety alarm. These are inexpensive and look like a key ring. The loud noise they make will attract the attention of passersby and frighten the bully off.

If you travel by train, avoid empty cars, and if you walk, don't walk alone. Leave earlier or later if necessary so you get there before the bully does, or so you can walk with friends.

◄ To avoid a bully, you could try taking a different route to and from school.

▲ It's a good idea not to wear headphones when you're walking out and about because it stops you from being aware of what is happening around you.

On the street

Sometimes a bully is someone you've never met before, who sees you on the street and decides to tease you or push you around. If possible, try to ignore the taunts and walk away as if you don't hear them. If the bullies become more threatening, or if it starts to get physical, yell loudly and get away fast. If they follow you, head for somewhere like a store or toward a group of people. If you're on a quiet street, run up to any door and knock loudly. Most bullies are afraid of being caught and will probably run away at this point. Tell the store manager or another adult what's happening. Don't leave until you're certain it's safe or you have called someone to get a ride home.

Top Tip!

Remove the bait! It's best not to carry or use (or at least let people see you are carrying) expensive cell phones or MP3 players when you're out. If bullies see this they might try to break them, steal them, or use them.

Getting help from others

Having tactics for dealing with bullies is useful and often helpful, but the real solution is to tell an adult. This is the single most important thing you can do. Keeping things secret is the bullies' biggest weapon. Getting help from others is yours.

▶ Bullies thrive on secrecy. Telling people and getting help from others is like taking the wind out of their sails or pulling the plug on their power.

Suffering in silence

Why do so many young people who are bullied never tell anyone? Some fear that they will upset their parents or worry that their parents will make a scene at school. Some don't think adults will understand or do anything about it. Some worry that if they tell, the bully will get angrier and the bullying will just get worse, or they think that people will think they are weak if they admit to being bullied. In fact, talking takes courage and telling an adult is the bravest thing you can do. Nobody can do anything to help you unless you tell someone about the bullying. The last thing you should do is to suffer in silence.

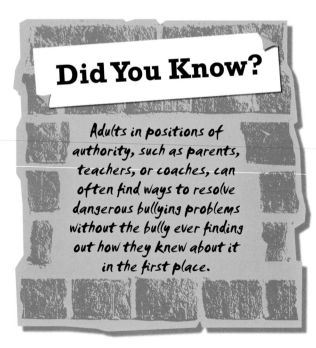

Did You Know?

Adults in positions of authority, such as parents, teachers, or coaches, can often find ways to resolve dangerous bullying problems without the bully ever finding out how they knew about it in the first place.

Top Tip!

Reporting a bully does NOT make you a tattletale. Bullying is serious and should be stopped. By reporting a bully you help yourself and others—from those who see bullying happen and feel scared to those the bully might target after you, if they think they can get away with it.

Who should I tell?

Tell someone you trust, like a parent, older sibling, or teacher. If you're not quite ready to tell an adult yet, start by telling a good friend. They probably won't be able to do anything about the bullying, but talking it through should help. You can see things more clearly when they are out in the open. And when you've said it out loud once it'll be easier to talk about it to an adult who can take action.

Friends and buddies

If the bullying happens at school, any of your teachers or the principal should be able to help. If you don't want to talk to a teacher (or even a parent) alone, perhaps a friend could go with you or speak to the adult on your behalf. Some schools have peer support (or "buddy") systems. Peer supporters are young people you can talk to who are trained to help other young people with their concerns, and figure out how to deal with them.

◄ Telling people about the bullying can feel like getting a massive weight off your chest!

Tips for telling

There's not a right or wrong way to tell people about bullying. Sometimes it might just burst out of you suddenly when you can't take it anymore. But it may help to plan what you're going to say.

A time to talk

When you've decided who to tell, figure out when it's best to talk to them. You might prefer to pick a quiet time when you won't be interrupted or when the adult isn't tired or stressed, such as after younger children are in bed and the dishes are done. Think about what you want out of the conversation. Do you just want them to listen to you, or do you want them to devise a plan with you? Tell them before you begin.

Did You Know?

Bottling up your feelings is bad for you. If you're not quite sure how to talk about the bullying, write down what's been happening to you. Then, give it to an adult you trust to read.

You could say something like "I've got something really important to tell you, but I need you to sit quietly while I get it all out. I also need you to promise you won't do anything about it without talking to me first."

◀ Aside from telling adults the facts, tell them how upset you are by the bullying. It's important that they know how much the bullying is hurting you.

Talking to teachers

When you talk about bullying with a teacher, it helps to be prepared. You could make and show them notes about what has happened to you, where it happened, how often it happened, who was involved, and who saw it happening. If you've kept a diary about the bullying, you could show them that, too. When you tell a teacher about being bullied, they should listen to you and take your problem seriously. They should never dismiss your concerns.

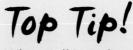

Top Tip!

When talking about bullying, it pays to tell the whole truth and nothing but the truth. If you exaggerate and someone discovers that a little bit of it wasn't true, they might give the bully the benefit of the doubt. All bullying is bad—you don't need to exaggerate the facts.

The teacher should tell you what will happen next and what they are going to do about it. If these things don't happen, talk to another teacher, or the principal, perhaps taking a parent with you. They can help find the right people to help you, as well as continuing to support you themselves.

◄ If you have kept a record of bullying incidents, you can let your diary show the teacher what has happened.

Taking it further

Bullying can sometimes stop quickly when you get help. If it doesn't, or if the first person you speak to cannot help you, keep asking different people until you find someone who does something to fix the problem. Tell and keep telling.

Calling for help

What if you don't feel there is an adult who will take action to help you, or what if the adults who should help you are the problem? You could try talking to an adult from elsewhere, such as your church or gym, or you could go to the police. Many people also visit websites and hotlines that have counselors who help young people who are in trouble or danger. Some of these are listed at the end of this book. They are free and confidential and they help many young people every year.

▲ Sometimes it's easier to talk to someone you don't know. Hotline counselors are trained and have experience in dealing with problems like bullying so they will be able to advise you on what to do in your particular situation.

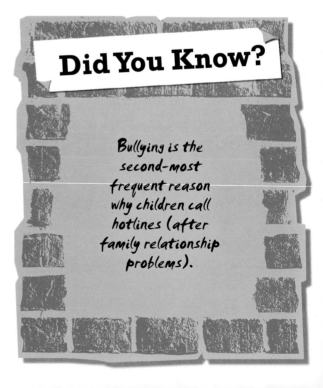

Did You Know?

Bullying is the second-most frequent reason why children call hotlines (after family relationship problems).

Talking to a counselor

You could also try talking to a counselor to help with the emotional upset caused by bullying. Counselors give people a chance to talk about their feelings and help them figure out what to do and how to go about it. Just like going to the doctor for advice about a physical problem, counselors can help you deal with emotional issues.

Never give up

Sometimes bullying makes people so desperate and depressed that they can see no way out of it and can't imagine anyone will ever be able to help them. Some victims have harmed themselves and others have even taken their own lives. It's really hard to imagine there is a way out when you are so very unhappy and everything seems bleak, but please never, ever give up. Keep asking for help. There is always a solution.

▲ Many people who have been bullied say that they don't feel better right away. It takes time to recover from bullying. Some say the experience of dealing with a bully gave them the strength to succeed and be happy—and to prove just how wrong the bullies were!

Ban the bullying

Everyone has a right to feel and to be safe, and we should all do what we can to ban bullying. There are some things we can all do to show bullies that we know and all agree that bullying is unacceptable.

Don't stand by

If you see someone being bullied, there is a lot you can do. You can refuse to stand and watch, or smile or laugh when someone is being bullied. This just gives the bully an audience and urges them on. You could tell the bully to stop and try to encourage others around you to do the same, if you feel safe doing so. If you fear this might make the bully turn and attack you too, walk away and go and tell a teacher or adult what's happening. Then perhaps you could talk to the target of the bullying to show them that they are not alone.

YOU CAN DO IT!

You can help others who are bullied by reaching out to them. Ask them to join a game, ask them if they are OK, or sit with them at lunchtime. This might seem like a small thing to do, but it can stop people from feeling alone and show them that some people know what the bully is doing is wrong.

▶ Never put yourself in danger. If you see someone fighting or arguing, never step in to stop it. Instead, go and get help.

What schools can do

All schools must have an anti-bullying policy. This means they should have a plan for how to prevent and deal with all forms of bullying among students. This is vital for the safety and happiness of all students and to show bullies that bullying won't be tolerated. There are other things schools can do, too. Schools can hold special weeks, workshops, or assemblies about bullying. School councils could organize questionnaires to ask all students what bullying problems they know about. Some schools have websites where people can report bullying online so there is no chance of the bully tracing it back to them. What does your school do and what could it do better?

Did You Know?

Even presidents speak out against bullying. In 2012 President Barack Obama said: "It's wrong, it's disruptive, and we can all prevent it. We've all got more work to do. Everyone has to take action against bullying."

The last word...

No one should be bullied and bullying should not be and does not have to be a normal part of childhood. All forms of bullying are harmful to the bully, the target, and the people who see it happen. We should all work together and we should never give up trying to challenge or stop bullying.

▼ We all need to make a stand together to say "No" to bullying.

Quiz

Try this quiz to find out how good you are at knowing different types of bullying and how to tackle them. Are you ready to say no to bullying or do you need to recap on a few key points first?

1 You are playing football and someone accidentally kicks you and it really hurts. Do you…
 a Kick them back as hard as you can
 b Shout for the referee and cry
 c Give them a chance to apologize

2 You are walking to school and three bullies demand your lunch money and cell phone. Do you…
 a Try to fight them to get your things back
 b Push them and try to run away
 c Give them the money and phone and tell a teacher as soon as you get to school

3 A friend runs you down the whole time, makes you feel bad for seeing other people, and makes you do things you don't want to. Do you…
 a Stay friends with them because they're cool and you're scared of them
 b Stay friends with them because you can't believe anyone else would want to be your friend
 c Try to find some real friends

4 A bully tries to exclude you from a game that other friends are playing. Do you…
 a Hang around and try to spoil the game for everyone else
 b Sit alone in a corner feeling very hurt and upset
 c Be persistent and keep giving reasons why you should play until they let you join in

5 One day at school someone who's never spoken to you before makes a nasty comment about the way you look. Do you…
 a Yell back and threaten to punch them
 b Think about it all day and start to feel self-conscious about the feature that was criticized
 c Ignore it because it's the first time it's happened, but vow to tell a teacher if it happens again

6 Someone sends you an abusive text. Do you…
- **a** Send them back an even ruder text telling them exactly what you think of them
- **b** Keep reading and rereading it until you feel really miserable
- **c** Save it so you can print it later if need be, but then delete it from your inbox so you don't have to read it again

7 Someone is bullying you on your way to school each morning. Do you…
- **a** Tell your mom you're sick and stop going to school
- **b** Arrive at school an hour late every day rather than risk meeting them
- **c** Take a different route or get a ride with friends to avoid them

8 An older bully is hitting a classmate in front of a crowd. Do you…
- **a** Ignore it and quietly sneak away, grateful you're not the target
- **b** Stand by feeling helpless, watching the beating
- **c** Get help or try to stop the bully yourself—if you can do so without getting hurt

9 You tell a teacher you've been bullied for weeks, but they just tell you to ignore it. Do you…
- **a** Moan to a friend about what a lousy teacher they are
- **b** Feel even more helpless and decide there is nothing else you can do about it
- **c** Tell another teacher or the principal and ask a parent to come with you to meet them and talk about the problem

10 You are being bullied at school. What's the most important thing to do?
- **a** Keep quiet—you're not a snitch who tells on other people
- **b** Keep quiet—if you say anything the bullying will get worse
- **c** Tell a teacher, your parents, and anyone else who'll listen—bullies thrive on secrecy and taking that away from them is vital

Answers

Mostly As… Bullying makes you angry and it should. The problem is that sometimes you might be putting yourself at risk when you fight back. Recap the chapters about dealing with bullies and getting help from others, and you'll soon have it covered.

Mostly Bs… You are getting there. You just need a little more confidence in yourself and your power to make a change. Read through the chapters about dealing with bullies and practice those techniques some more.

Mostly Cs… You've got it! You have the skills and techniques to say a loud and clear "NO" to bullying. Get out there and use them, to protect yourself and others from the badness that is bullying.

Find out more

Books

Beating the Bullies: How Did Ben Help Himself?
by Dr. Lucy Blunt (Curry Publishing, 2013)
A guide for children ages 7–11 including strategies
for coping with bullying.

Best of Friends, Best of Enemies
by Brian Moses (Wayland, 2011)
A collection of poems showing how to cope with good and bad
acquaintances. One half deals with bullies and bullying; the second
half is dedicated to poems about friends and friendship.

Bullies, Bigmouths and So-called Friends
by Jenny Alexander (Hodder, 2006)
This book uses an entertaining mix of exercises, quizzes,
and fictional scenarios to help readers build up their self-esteem.

Cyber Bullying (Hot Topics) by Nick Hunter (Raintree, 2012)
This book helps young people address the specific issue
of cyberbullying.

Teen Life Confidential: Bullies, Cyberbullies and Frenemies
by Michele Elliot (Wayland, 2013)
This is a guide about what bullying is, where it happens,
and what you can do about it.

Websites and hotlines

www.stopbullying.gov
A federal government website managed by the U.S. Department of Health & Human Services. This site provides one-stop access to U.S. Government information on bullying topics. Information on cyberbullying can be found at **www.stopbullying.gov/cyberbullying**.

www.pacerkidsagainstbullying.org
Provided by PACER's National Bullying Prevention Center, it is a creative, innovative, and educational website designed for elementary school students to learn about bullying prevention, engage in activities, and be inspired to take action. For middle and high school students, visit **www.pacerteensagainstbullying.org**, which is a site created by and for teens to address bullying, to take action, and to be heard.

www.stompoutbullying.org
This is a national anti-bullying and cyberbullying organization for kids and teens. The website provides information, news, and support.

www.stopcyberbullying.org
This website is an interactive resource, delivering information on cyberbullying for kids and teens.

STOMP Out Bullying Help Chat Line
Call the hotline for help, or visit the link below to chat online with trained volunteers.
Call: 855-790-HELP (4357)
Chat: www.stompoutbullying.org/livechat.php

BRAVEline
A hotline launched by the United Federation of Teachers. It's called BRAVE, which stands for "building respect, acceptance, and voice through education." You can call, text, or chat online with counselors.
Call: 212-709-3222
Text: 646-490-0233
Chat: www.uft.org/our-rights/brave

Index